IT'S TIME TO EAT PARSLEY

It's Time to Eat PARSLEY

Walter the Educator

Silent King Books
A WhichHead Entertainment Imprint

Copyright © 2025 by Walter the Educator

All rights reserved. No part of this book may be reproduced in any manner whatsoever without written per- mission except in the case of brief quotations embodied in critical articles and reviews.

First Printing, 2024

Disclaimer

This book is a literary work; the story is not about specific persons, locations, situations, and/or circumstances unless mentioned in a historical context. Any resemblance to real persons, locations, situations, and/or circumstances is coincidental. This book is for entertainment and informational purposes only. The author and publisher offer this information without warranties expressed or implied. No matter the grounds, neither the author nor the publisher will be accountable for any losses, injuries, or other damages caused by the reader's use of this book. The use of this book acknowledges an understanding and acceptance of this disclaimer.

It's Time to Eat PARSLEY is a collectible early learning book by Walter the Educator suitable for all ages belonging to Walter the Educator's Time to Eat Book Series. Collect more books at WaltertheEducator.com

USE THE EXTRA SPACE TO TAKE NOTES AND DOCUMENT YOUR MEMORIES

PARSLEY

It's time to eat, hooray, hooray!

It's Time to Eat
Parsley

A special herb is here today!

With curly leaves or smooth and bright,

Parsley is a tasty sight!

It grows so green in garden beds,

With little stems and leafy heads.

Pick some fresh and hold it near,

Its smell is strong and full of cheer!

We wash it well and shake it dry,

The water splashes, oh, oh my!

A little shake, a little spin,

Now it's clean and fresh again!

We chop it up so nice and small,

Tiny bits, don't let them fall!

Into a bowl or on a plate,

Parsley makes our dinner great!

It's Time to Eat
Parsley

Sprinkle, sprinkle, what a treat!

It makes our food taste fresh and sweet.

On veggies, fish, or warm mashed peas,

It adds a flavor sure to please!

In soups and stews, it swirls around,

Or in a salad, crisp and sound.

Even in a smoothie bright,

It makes each bite just taste so right!

Parsley helps us feel so strong,

It keeps us healthy all day long!

Packed with goodness, bright and green,

One of the best herbs ever seen!

Take a nibble, taste and see,

It's fresh and yummy, just for me!

Not too spicy, not too sweet,

It's Time to Eat
Parsley

Parsley is a snack so neat!

So when you see these leaves so fine,

Pick some up, it's dinner time!

A little here, a little there,

Parsley adds a touch of care!

Now we're full and feeling great,

Parsley's magic fills our plate!

So fresh, so bright, so fun to chew,

It's Time to Eat
Parsley

Try some parsley, it's good for you!

ABOUT THE CREATOR

Walter the Educator is one of the pseudonyms for Walter Anderson. Formally educated in Chemistry, Business, and Education, he is an educator, an author, a diverse entrepreneur, and he is the son of a disabled war veteran. "Walter the Educator" shares his time between educating and creating. He holds interests and owns several creative projects that entertain, enlighten, enhance, and educate, hoping to inspire and motivate you. Follow, find new works, and stay up to date with Walter the Educator™ at WaltertheEducator.com

www.ingramcontent.com/pod-product-compliance
Lightning Source LLC
LaVergne TN
LVHW052013060526
838201LV00059B/4017

IT'S TIME TO EAT CHIMICHANGAS

It's Time to Eat CHIMICHANGAS

Walter the Educator

Silent King Books
A WhichHead Entertainment Imprint

Copyright © 2025 by Walter the Educator

All rights reserved. No part of this book may be reproduced in any manner whatsoever without written per- mission except in the case of brief quotations embodied in critical articles and reviews.

First Printing, 2024

Disclaimer

This book is a literary work; the story is not about specific persons, locations, situations, and/or circumstances unless mentioned in a historical context. Any resemblance to real persons, locations, situations, and/or circumstances is coincidental. This book is for entertainment and informational purposes only. The author and publisher offer this information without warranties expressed or implied. No matter the grounds, neither the author nor the publisher will be accountable for any losses, injuries, or other damages caused by the reader's use of this book. The use of this book acknowledges an understanding and acceptance of this disclaimer.

It's Time to Eat CHIMICHANGAS is a collectible early learning book by Walter the Educator suitable for all ages belonging to Walter the Educator's Time to Eat Book Series. Collect more books at WaltertheEducator.com

USE THE EXTRA SPACE TO TAKE NOTES AND DOCUMENT YOUR MEMORIES

CHIMICHANGAS

It's time to eat, hooray, hooray!

It's Time to Eat
Chimichangas

Chimichangas on my tray.

Crispy, golden, piping hot,

I can't wait to eat a lot!

Cheesy, beefy, full of spice,

Every bite is oh-so-nice.

Rolled up tight and fried just right,

A yummy treat for my delight!

I take a fork, I take a bite,

Oh, this taste is such a sight!

Crunchy outside, soft within,

Where should I even begin?

Dip it here and dip it there,

Sour cream and guac to share!

Maybe salsa, just a drop,

Spicy fun, oh, please don't stop!

It's Time to Eat
Chimichangas

Mom and Dad take bites so big,

Brother does a happy jig.

Sister smiles and says, "Oh wow!

I want another, right now!"

Chew it slowly, don't go fast,

Make this chimichanga last.

Savor every tasty chew,

There's enough for me and you!

But oh no! My plate is bare,

Not a single bite is there.

Every piece is gone away,

Let's make more, hip hip hooray!

Back to the kitchen, here we go,

Rolling, frying, nice and slow.

Golden brown and smelling sweet,

It's Time to Eat
Chimichangas

Once again, it's time to eat!

Chimichangas, oh so neat,

Crispy, tasty, fun to eat.

Every dinner, every night,

They're my favorite, what a sight!

Now my tummy's full and tight,

Time to say a big goodnight.

Dreaming of my favorite treat,

It's Time to Eat
Chimichangas

Chimichangas, can't be beat!

ABOUT THE CREATOR

Walter the Educator is one of the pseudonyms for Walter Anderson. Formally educated in Chemistry, Business, and Education, he is an educator, an author, a diverse entrepreneur, and he is the son of a disabled war veteran. "Walter the Educator" shares his time between educating and creating. He holds interests and owns several creative projects that entertain, enlighten, enhance, and educate, hoping to inspire and motivate you. Follow, find new works, and stay up to date with Walter the Educator™

at WaltertheEducator.com

www.ingramcontent.com/pod-product-compliance
Lightning Source LLC
LaVergne TN
LVHW052011060526
838201LV00059B/3967